W9-AVK-495

JOLIET PUBLIC LIBRARY

First Facts®

Transportation Zone

Buses

in Action

by Allison Lassieur

CAPSTONE PRESS
a capstone imprint

First Facts is published by Capstone Press,
1710 Roe Crest Drive, North Mankato, Minnesota 56003.
www.capstonepub.com

Copyright © 2012 by Capstone Press, a Capstone imprint.
All rights reserved.
No part of this publication may be reproduced in whole or in part, or stored in a
retrieval system, or transmitted in any form or by any means, electronic, mechanical,
photocopying, recording, or otherwise, without written permission of the publisher.
For information regarding permission, write to Capstone Press,
1710 Roe Crest Drive, North Mankato, Minnesota 56003.

Books published by Capstone Press are manufactured with paper
containing at least 10 percent post-consumer waste.

Library of Congress Cataloging-in-Publication Data
Lassieur, Allison.
  Buses in action / by Allison Lassieur.
      p. cm.—(First facts. Transportation zone)
  Includes bibliographical references and index.
  Summary: "Describes buses, including their history, their parts, how they work, and
how people use them to travel"—Provided by publisher.
  ISBN 978-1-4296-7689-2 (library binding)
  ISBN 978-1-4296-7966-4 (paperback)
  1. Buses—Juvenile literature. 2. Bus travel—Juvenile literature. I. Title.
  TL232.L37 2012
  388.3'4233—dc23   2011029173

Editorial Credits
Carrie Braulick Sheely, editor; Sarah Bennett and Lori Bye, designers;
    Eric Gohl, media researcher; Kathy McColley, production specialist

Image Credits
Art Resource, N.Y./Scala, 12
BigStockPhoto.com/Vicki France, cover
iStockphoto/Hulton Archive, 15; Jaap2, 6
Library of Congress, 17
Newscom/ZUMA Press/Dan Trevan, 9; m11, 11
Shutterstock/Chris Jenner, 18; Lusoimages, 21; Michael Rubin, 5;
Tupungato, 1

3 1967 01240 2957

Printed in the United States of America in North Mankato, Minnesota.

102011   006405CGS12

Table of Contents

Buses

A bus comes to a quick stop along a busy city street. Some passengers shuffle off the bus, and others swiftly get on the bus. Soon the bus takes off to continue its **route**.

Buses are a common sight in cities throughout the world. They are an easy, cheap way for people to travel. Buses carry many people at one time. Without them, many city streets would become clogged with traffic.

route: the course followed to get somewhere

Traveling on a City Bus

Many buses travel routes in cities. People wait for these buses at bus stops. A sign on the bus tells people where the bus is going. People pay **fares** to ride the bus.

Passengers signal when they want to get off the bus. They push buttons or pull cords that ring a bell.

fare: the cost of riding a bus

7

Parts of a Bus

A bus' design depends on its use. But most buses have the same main parts. An engine powers the bus and makes the wheels turn. A bus has many large windows. One or more doors are on a bus' side. The driver opens and closes the doors. A fare box is next to the driver. Some passengers relax in roomy seats. Others stand and hold onto poles or handles.

How a Bus Works

Buses generally work the same. A bus driver flips a switch to start the engine. Many bus engines use **diesel fuel** to produce power. Others use gasoline or liquefied **petroleum** gas (LPG). The driver uses an accelerator and a brake pedal to control the bus' speed and to stop the bus. A steering wheel turns the bus.

diesel fuel: a heavy oil that burns to make power; diesel fuel is heavier than gasoline

petroleum: raw material for fuel oil found underground; petroleum is processed into a variety of chemicals

12

Before the Bus

People walked, rode horses, or rode in **carriages** before buses were invented. Carriages only held a few people at one time. City streets became crowded with carriages. People began to look for new ways to travel within cities.

carriage: a vehicle with wheels that is usually pulled by horses

Inventor of the Bus

Blaise Pascal invented the bus in Paris, France, in 1662. He hitched a team of horses to a large wagon. He called his invention an omnibus. The omnibus could carry more people than any carriage could. Eight passengers could ride in the first omnibus.

OMNIBUS

PADDINGTON to the BANK

DIORAMA REGENTS PARK

15

Early Buses

In 1819 omnibus service started throughout New York City and Paris. Soon many people began to call the vehicles buses.

In the early 1890s, people began driving gasoline-powered automobiles. Gasoline-powered buses first appeared in Germany. To make these buses, cars were lengthened. Other early buses that ran on gasoline were built on truck frames. By the 1930s, buses looked like modern buses.

17

15

St Paul's Cathedral
Fleet Street
Aldwych

TRAFALGAR SQUARE

15

RM1941

TURN TO OPEN

Buses around the World

Today many types of buses are used around the world. Double-decker buses have two levels. Passengers can sit on the top level or on the bottom level. Some buses look like two buses joined together. People travel on sightseeing buses when they visit new places. School buses bring students to and from school. Buses will continue to be an easy, dependable way to travel.

Bus Facts

- Several countries use trolley coaches. These vehicles look like buses. But they are powered by electric cables above streets.

- One early bus design had a large truck that pulled a trailer.

- The first buses in the United States carried 12 passengers.

- People in U.S. cities ride buses more than any other form of public transportation.

- More than 4.5 billion passengers ride U.S. city buses each year.

- A passenger rides a city bus an average of 4 miles (6 kilometers) each trip.

trolley coach

Hands On: Bus Routes

Buses follow routes. A bus route map will tell you which bus to take. On this map each bus route is a different color. You can practice finding routes on maps.

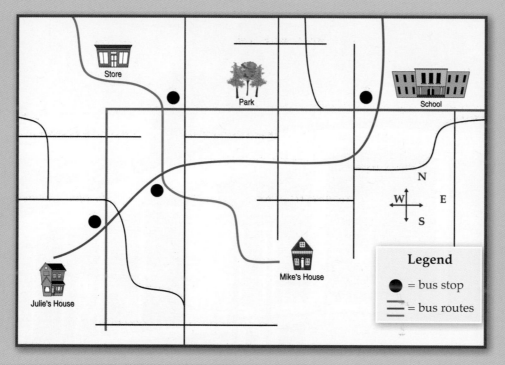

1. Find Julie's house on the map.
2. Find the school on the map.
3. Find the bus route that goes from Julie's house to the school without changing buses.
4. Find the route that goes from Mike's house to the store.
5. Find the routes that go from Julie's house to the park. Which one would you take?

Glossary

accelerator (ak-sel-uh-RAY-tor)—a pedal that controls how fast a vehicle travels

carriage (KAYR-ij)—a vehicle with wheels that is usually pulled by horses

diesel fuel (DEE-zuhl FYOOL)—a heavy oil that burns to make power

engine (EN-juhn)—a machine that makes the power needed to move something

fare (FAYR)—the cost of riding a bus

passenger (PASS-uhn-jur)—someone other than the driver who travels by bus or other form of transportation

petroleum (puh-TROH-lee-uhm)—raw material for fuel oil found underground; petroleum is processed into a variety of chemicals including gasoline, kerosene, and natural gas

route (ROUT)—the course followed to get somewhere

Read More

Peppas, Lynn. *Big Buses.* Vehicles on the Move. New York: Crabtree Pub., 2011.

Tourville, Amanda Doering. *Transportation in the City.* My Community. Mankato, Minn.: Capstone Press, 2011.

Internet Sites

FactHound offers a safe, fun way to find Internet sites related to this book. All of the sites on FactHound have been researched by our staff.

Here's all you do:

Visit *www.facthound.com*

Type in this code: 9781429676892

 Check out projects, games and lots more at
www.capstonekids.com

Index